WHAT'S ON
MyPlate?

T0080612

GET MOVING!

by Mari Schuh
Consulting editor: Gail Saunders-Smith, PhD

Consultant: Barbara J. Rolls, PhD
Guthrie Chair in Nutrition
Pennsylvania State University
University Park, Pennsylvania

CAPSTONE PRESS
a capstone imprint

Pebble Plus is published by Capstone Press,
1710 Roe Crest Drive, North Mankato, Minnesota 56003.
www.capstonepub.com

Library of Congress Cataloging-in-Publication Data
Schuh, Mari C., 1975–
  Get moving! / by Mari Schuh.
    p. cm.—(Pebble plus. What's on myplate?)
  Includes bibliographical references and index.
  Summary: "Simple text and photos describe USDA's MyPlate tool and healthy activity choices
for children"—Provided by publisher.
  ISBN 978-1-4296-8747-8 (library binding)
  ISBN 978-1-4296-9414-8 (paperback)
  ISBN 978-1-62065-326-5 (eBook PDF)
  ISBN 978-1-4765-3059-8 (e-book)

  1. Physical fitness for children—Juvenile literature. 2. Exercise for children—Juvenile literature. I. Title.
RJ133.S36 2013
613.7'1083—dc23   2012009314

Editorial Credits
Jeni Wittrock, editor; Gene Bentdahl, designer; Svetlana Zhurkin, media researcher; Kathy McColley,
    production specialist; Sarah Schuette, photo stylist; Marcy Morin, studio scheduler.

Photo Credits
All photos by Capstone Studio/Karon Dubke except:
Alamy: Enigma, 21; Dreamstime: Fototaras, 22 (middle left); iStockphotos: Christopher Futcher, 11, Judy Barranco,
22 (top right); Shutterstock: Monkey Business Images, 13, 22 (top middle), R. Gino Santa Maria, cover, spotmatik,
19, Volodymyr Krasyuk, back cover (left), 1; USDA, cover (inset), 9

Information in this book supports the
U.S. Department of Agriculture (USDA)'s
MyPlate food guidance system
found at *www.choosemyplate.gov*.
The USDA recommends that children
ages 6–17 "should do 60 minutes or more
of physical activity each day. Most of the
60 minutes should be either moderate- or
vigorous-intensity aerobic physical activity
and should include vigorous-intensity
physical activity at least 3 days a week."
The U.S. Department of Agriculture
(USDA) does not endorse any products,
services, or organizations.

Note to Parents and Teachers

The What's on MyPlate? series supports national science standards related to health and
nutrition. This book describes and illustrates the USDA's MyPlate exercise recommendations.
The images support early readers in understanding the text. The repetition of words and phrases
helps early readers learn new words. This book also introduces early readers to subject-specific
vocabulary words, which are defined in the Glossary section. Early readers may need assistance
to read some words and to use the Table of Contents, Glossary, Read More, Internet Sites, and
Index sections of the book.

Printed in the United States   5188

Table
of Contents

Let's Be Active 4

MyPlate 8

Get Moving 10

Ways to Get Moving 22

Glossary 23

Read More 23

Internet Sites 24

Index 24

Let's Be Active

Let's get off the couch

and have some fun!

How have you

been active today?

Playing, moving your body, and exercising help you stay healthy. Being active makes you feel good about yourself.

MyPlate

Exercising is a part of MyPlate. MyPlate is a tool that helps you eat right and stay active.

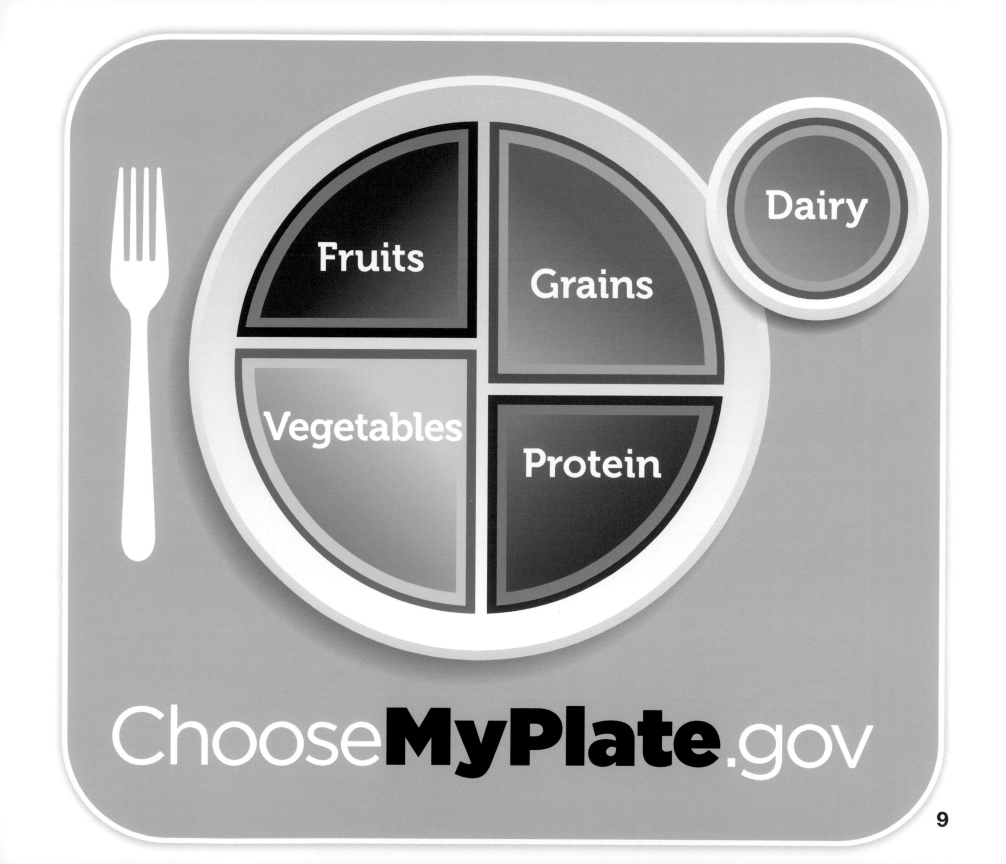

Get Moving

Play hard! Kids need to be active 60 minutes every day. Try to move more and sit less.

Get moving outside.

Go on a nature hike.

What do you see

and hear?

Take a ride on a swing
or play tag. Have fun
at the playground
with your friends.

Why not shoot some hoops after school? Grab a ball and get your heart pumping.

Pedal hard.

Enjoy a bike ride

with your family.

Staying active keeps you healthy and fit.

Let's get moving!

Ways to Get Moving

Kids need to be active at least 60 minutes every day. Here are some ways to get moving. How else can you be active?

swimming

jumping rope

in-line skating

dancing

soccer

running

biking

martial arts

playing catch

Glossary

active—being busy and moving around

exercise—physical activity you do to keep fit

healthy—being fit and well

hike—a long walk

MyPlate—a food plan that reminds people to eat healthful food and be active; MyPlate was created by the U.S. Department of Agriculture

Read More

Borgert-Spaniol, Megan. *Keeping Fit.* Eating Right with MyPlate. Minneapolis: Bellwether Media, 2012.

Heron, Jackie. *Let's Move in the Outdoors.* Move and Get Healthy! Minneapolis: Magic Wagon, 2012.

Tourville, Amanda Doering. *Get up and Go: Being Active.* How to Be Healthy! Minneapolis: Picture Window Books, 2009.

Internet Sites

FactHound offers a safe, fun way to find Internet sites related to this book. All of the sites on FactHound have been researched by our staff.

Here's all you do:

Visit *www.facthound.com*

Type in this code: 9781429687478

 Check out projects, games and lots more at **www.capstonekids.com**

Index

being active, 4, 6, 8, 10, 20, 22

biking, 18

daily recommendation, 10

exercising, 6, 8

feeling good, 6

health, 6, 20

hiking, 12

MyPlate, 8

playing, 6, 10

tag, 14

Word Count: 134
Grade: 1
Early-Intervention Level: 14